Diamonas In The Rough

From Pieces to Peace to your Ordained Destiny and Purpose

By YolandaWashngton Cowan

Unless otherwise noted, all Scripture is taken from the (NLT) New Living Translation of the Bible or (KJV) King James Version.

Diamonds In the Rough: From Pieces to Peace to your Ordained Destiny and Purpose

Copyright @ 2018
by Yolanda Washington-Cowan
ISBN-13:978-0999777626
ISBN-10:0999777629

All rights reserved
Published by
B-Inspired Publishing
7285 Winchester Road, Suite 109
Memphis, TN 38125
www.B-Inspiredpub.com
Printed in the United States
First Edition: February 2018

All rights reserved under International Copyright Law. Contents and/or cover may not be reproduced in whole or in part in any form without the expressed written consent of the Publisher.

Table of Contents

INTRODUCTION 1
CHAPTER ONE 6
  THE COUNTERFEIT DIAMOND 6
CHAPTER TWO 16
  THE CLOUDY DIAMOND 16
    Inclusions 16
    Fluorescence 17
    Dirt 18
    Cracks 20
CHAPTER THREE 24
  THE DIAMOND NEEDLE 24
    JEPHTHAH: FROM SHAME TO HEROISM 24
    JOHN MARK: GEM FROM THE FURNACE OF DISAGREEMENT 26
    ONESIMUS: MY SON IN BOND 27
CHAPTER FOUR 32
  THE FEATHER DIAMOND 32
    Sarah 33
    Moses 34
    Rahab 34
    Peter 35

CHAPTER FIVE 38

  THE DIAMOND CHIP 38

CHAPTER SIX 42

  A CRACKED DIAMOND 42

CHAPTER SEVEN 47

  THE TWINNING WISP 48

CHAPTER EIGHT 52

  THE CERTIFIED DIAMOND: DIAMOND THAT HAS RECEIVED SALVATION 52

CHAPTER NINE 56

  THE TRANSFORMED DIAMOND: THE REFILLING OF THE HOLY SPIRIT 56

    Growing in the word of God 57

    Building a daily prayer relationship with God 61

    Fellowshipping in the house of the Lord 62

    Serving God 63

    Teaching and Discipleship 65

    Walking in love 66

CHAPTER TEN 70

  SHINE LIKE A DIAMOND: THE PURPOSEFUL DIAMOND 70

Here are some things that the Bible tells us about work: 74

The 4 C's 81

First C- Cut 81

Second C- Color... 82

Third C- Clarity 83

Fourth C- Carat Weight..................................... 84

CHAPTER ELEVEN... 87

PRAYERS 87

LORD SHOW ME MY PURPOSE........................ 87

A PRAYER OF GUIDANCE TO START A NEW DAY 89

PRAYERS FOR INNER HEALING 91

BIBLIOGRAPHY 94

NOTES.. 95

ACKNOWLEDGEMENTS

A special thanks to my husband, Vaughn Cowan, my mother Delores and son Kenneth, Jr for their love, support, and encouragement.

Also, thanks to Patricia Givens-Perry and Wendy Oliver for editing and proofreading, and having patience in assisting me with this book.

INTRODUCTION

Diamond is a rare, naturally occurring mineral. It is the hardest known natural substance. It is used as a cutting tool and for other uses where durability is required.

No optical eye can accurately tell the various grades of diamond, some are of higher quality than others. Judging the value of a diamond in the rough is an onerous task. The process is nebulous, no one can tell if it is of great value or worthless, if subjected to the cutting process.

Accurate evaluation of a diamond cannot be haphazardly done. It entails having a great level of skill and expertise. Also, shaping it to different desired awesome gems we so anticipate is largely hinged on having an appropriate facility and using the right tools.

Pathetically, a number of us have incessantly evaluated and wrongly judged people around us, including ourselves, using wrong parameters of evaluations. The truth is, none of us is a worthy judge. What the creator of the universe has embedded in us is too complex for any mortal to rationalize or quantify. Many of the commentaries we run about people are mere attempts to air our opinions of ignorance. Although, we all have rights to our opinions, but only the counsel of the Lord will stand.

While living a life of promiscuity, was it not easy to envisage the eternal doom of Rahab the harlot? When Jesus sent them without script direction and purse funds, was it not easy to describe how glorious the mansion of Judas Iscariot would be in heaven? Eventually, our predictions often show that we are men, not God.

Embroiled by our human naivety and ignorance, we wrongly categorize people into our self-schemed ranges and classes, probably because of their temporal weaknesses or strength. We often forget how ephemeral man and his characters can be.

Sincerely, we are all projects in progress. If the conclusion is drawn due to the level of completion, God has a humbling way of making man's truth become lies. The present rough surface of our diamond is not a perfect reflection of our potential and abilities. Abilities are not worn like clothes, each dawn and sunset gradually unveils it.

Truthfully, we are wonderfully made by God. We are not just worthy in God's eyes, He is also jealous over us. Graciously, His thoughts over us are thoughts of good to give us a future and a pleasant end. Interestingly, God's awesome desired end for us needs no human accreditation or support, because faithful is He who has promised.

If the greatest sacrifice of salvation was not too big for God to give to us, how much more, will He not freely make our rough diamonds priceless gemstones?

Diamonds In The Rough

Diamonds In The Rough

COUNTERFEIT DIAMOND

CHAPTER ONE

THE COUNTERFEIT DIAMOND

Some counterfeit diamonds are easily detected as substandard right off the bat. They may be advertised as faux gemstones, or you may see a stamp on the inside of the band of a ring that says C.Z., the abbreviation for Cubic Zirconia. Others, however, try to pass themselves off as the real thing. How can you tell the difference? Well, there are a number of tests that one can use to sort out the genuine from the fake.

Just like diamonds, some people try to pass themselves off as Christians when they are not. How do you keep from being fooled? Again, just like there are ways to test for a gemstone's authenticity, there are ways of differentiating the true Christian from the counterfeit.

> *Such people claim they know God, but they deny him by the way they live. They are detestable and disobedient, worthless for doing anything good.*
> ***(Titus 1:16)***

Have you ever known people who claim they are Christian, but you cannot see any evidence of regeneration in their lives? They attend church on Sunday, but live like the devil for the rest of the week. No one is perfect, the Bible tells us that **(Romans 3:10).** When people reduce their walk with God to mere lip services and claim that they are Christians, yet they consistently disobey God's commands and live a life of spiritual recklessness; if their fruits negate their claims, you can be sure that they are counterfeit Christians.

> *Beware of false prophets who come disguised as harmless sheep but are really vicious wolves. You can identify them by their fruit, that is, by the way they act. Can you pick grapes from thornbushes, or figs from thistles? A good tree produces good fruit, and a bad tree produces bad fruit...Yes, just as you can identify a tree by its fruit, so you can identify people by their actions.*
> **(Matthew 7:15-17; 20)**

Once in a while, a substandard gem is not only erroneously taken as the genuine article; it is used by someone to convince people of the validity of their claims and intentions. Similarly, there are some people who are not only counterfeit Christians; they try to purposely lead others astray. Again, we are admonished to pay careful attention to their lives. How do they act? What fruit are they producing? **Galatians 5:22** tells us what kind of fruit we should see.

> *But the Holy Spirit produces this kind of fruit in our lives: love, joy, peace, patience, kindness, goodness, faithfulness, gentleness, and self control.* **(Galatians 5:22)**

A true Christian will not try to confuse you or skew a lie to become truth.

> *Dear friends, do not believe everyone who claims to speak by the Spirit. You must test them to see if the spirit they have comes from God. For there are many false prophets in the world. This is how we know if they have the Spirit of God: If a person claiming to be a prophet acknowledges that Jesus Christ came in a real body, that person has the Spirit of God. But if someone claims to be a prophet and does not acknowledge the truth about*

> *Jesus, that person is not from God. Such a person has the spirit of the Antichrist, which you heard is coming into the world and indeed is already here. (1 John 4:1-3)*

It can be difficult to tell whether a stone is a true diamond or something else. Occasionally, you will need to have an expert examine the gem using an x-ray. The molecular structure of a true diamond is such that it won't even appear when x-rayed, while false gems such as cubic zirconium and other crystals are clearly visible in x-rays.

In the same way, it is sometimes necessary to look to see what is inside a person who is claiming to be a Christian. If a person calls himself a Christian, yet denies the truth of Jesus, it becomes obvious that they don't have the Spirit of God in them. Pathetically, there are many factions within the church who deny Jesus' humanity. However, Jesus is fully God and fully man.

> *For in Christ lives all the fullness of God in a human body. (Colossians 2:9)*

> *Jesus said... So now I am giving you a new commandment: Love each other. Just as I have loved you, you should love each other. Your love for one another will prove to the world that you are my disciples. (John 13:34-35)*

To know a true diamond, you should have a quality diamond with which to compare. One of the efficient ways to judge if a gemstone is truly a diamond is by weighing it against a known diamond of the same size and shape. Cubic zirconia weighs a little over 50% more than a diamond of the same basic size and shape. If you have nothing to compare it with, you'll have a hard time determining whether or not it is real.

Jesus gave us an example of the way we should live our lives by the way he lived His. We should love each other like Him. Isn't that's a tall order?

Jesus gave of His time. From that first recorded miracle when Jesus only wanted to enjoy the wedding of a friend, it is abundantly clear that Jesus prioritizes other people. **(John 2:1-11)**

In Matthew chapter 8, scripture revealed how He had been busy the whole day; teaching large crowds, healing the sick, casting out demons, and still, the crowds pressed in around him. When he finally left and tried to get a little rest as they sailed across the lake, a storm came up. His disciples woke Him because they were afraid.

Instead of rolling over and going back to sleep, Jesus woke up and calmed the storm. Jesus went off to be alone after hearing the awful news that his cousin had been executed, but the people found out where He was and followed Him there. Instead of getting angry or turning them away, Jesus had compassion on them and healed their sicknesses **(Matthew 14:13-14).** There are countless examples of miracles throughout Scripture. Just like Jesus, a true Christian will put others first.

He forgave Judas even when he knew he was going to betray him. He forgave those who crucified him. He knew what we were like, everything we had ever done or would ever do, yet,

> *But God showed his great love for us by sending Christ to die for us while we were still sinners. **(Romans 5:8)***

Not only did God send Christ to die for us, but Christ agreed. He had a full understanding of the pains and rigors He would endure. He could see the shame, suffering and rejection, but Christ went through with it. The perfect standard of measurement that can be employed in knowing a true believer from a false one, compare their lives with that of Christ.

Job scraped his skin with a piece of broken pottery as he sat among the ashes. His wife said to him, "Are you still trying to maintain your integrity? Curse God and die."

> *But Job replied, "You talk like a foolish woman. Should we accept only good things from the hand of God and never anything bad?" So in all this, Job said nothing wrong. **(Job 2:8-10)***

Another way to tell a true diamond from a counterfeit is by its hardness. A diamond is one of the hardest minerals on Earth. We have all watched movies where someone is able to cut glass with a diamond. Well, it's true; a diamond will scratch other materials without becoming scratched or damaged itself. There are stones which resemble diamonds, but they are much softer than diamonds. A white topaz, for instance, looks similar to a diamond, but it is not as durable. If you look closely near the facets of the gem, you may notice scratches. You would not see those in a real diamond; they are too hard.

When a true Christian is buffeted by the storms of life, they stand firm. They have the Spirit of God in them to keep them strong. God is not interested in "bread and butter" Christians, whose only reason of serving God is because of what God can do for them, not what they can do for His Kingdom. They are the species of Christian who give complaints, murmur incessantly and prefer to go back to Egypt over entering the land of promise. God cannot test them with the wilderness experiences, a den of lions or furnace of fire, because He knows their vulnerabilities and weaknesses. If someone has only the form of godliness but denies its power, we should stay away from them **(2 Timothy 3:5).**

If you have never read the story of Job, you might want to stop now and read it. This man had everything he could ever desire, family, friends, wealth, lofty position in the community, but Satan was allowed to test Job's faith. Nearly everything was taken from him. Disaster assailed him on every side. Calamity drenched him like torrential rainfall, pains pervaded his life and his wealth nosedived into obscurity. Through it all, he stood firm. He did not query God or blaspheme His Holy name. He was proactive in rebuking his wife for her erring advice. He accepted the good with the bad, knowing that God was in control.

Some people act 'good,' but when times get tough, they fold, shrink and burst. They don't have the Spirit of God in them. Their lives have not been built on the firm foundation of unwavering faith in God.

> *Anyone who listens to my teaching and follows it is wise, like a person who builds a house on solid rock. Though the rain comes in torrents and the floodwaters rise and the winds beat against that house, it won't collapse because it is built on bedrock.* ***(Matthew 7:24-25)***

> *They will be my people, and I will be their God. And I will give them one heart and one purpose: to worship me forever, for their own good and for the good of all their descendants. **(Jeremiah 32:38-39)***

A true follower of Christ will be forever changed by their experience and encounter with God. They will not serve God one minute, then the world the next. Their purpose is to serve the Lord, not to have the Lord serve them and their desires. The true believer does not just clean the outer life that people can see. He has a complete change of heart and their outward behavior changes, because their inward person has changed. They know how important it is to follow the Lord in spirit and in truth, so that their children will see how important God is to them.

> *There is only one thing worth being concerned about. Mary has discovered it, and it will not be taken away from her. **(Luke 10:42)***

Someone who wants to follow Christ will want to spend more time with Him, since we always have time for what we love. They will make time for Him, and it will be the most important thing in their lives; more important than screen time, busy work and 'good' things of our ephemeral world. In comparison to the things of God, everything loses its value.

> *For they don't understand God's way of making people right with himself. Refusing to accept God's way, they cling to their own way of getting right with God by trying to keep the law. **(Romans 10:3)***

Have you ever heard someone say, 'I'm a good person'? As if 'goodness' is the ticket to Heaven? God's word tells us that no one is good. Good enough is never good enough. If we were able to get into Heaven under our own power, there would be no need for Jesus' sacrifice.

*For the Son of Man came to seek and save those who are lost. **(Luke 19:10)***

Someone who genuinely seeks the Lord will admit that they are lost. They see the faults in their lives. They have no delusions that they are 'good enough.' They readily admit their need to be saved. Just as Zacchaeus promised to make restitution to those he had wronged, someone who is serious about following Christ will do what they can to make things right.

*The Kingdom of Heaven is like a treasure that a man discovered hidden in a field. In his excitement, he hid it again and sold everything he owned to get enough money to buy the field. **(Matthew 13:44)***

Have you ever searched a field with a metal detector? You may have found a few coins or a lost button. What if you ran across a real treasure? What would you do, especially if that field didn't belong to you? What would you be willing to give up in order to obtain the new treasure? How much more valuable is the Kingdom of Heaven? The beauty and royalty of heaven is indescribable. The man in this scripture **Matthew 13:44** sold everything he owned so that he could buy that field and get that treasure.

If a person truly wishes to follow Jesus, they will be willing to sacrifice much because they know that in the end, He is what really matters.

CLOUDY DIAMOND

CHAPTER TWO

THE CLOUDY DIAMOND

What is the most striking thing that you love about a diamond? Most likely, your answer is, sparkle and brilliance. Most people don't think about a diamond that is cloudy. After all, diamonds are supposed to be bright and dazzling. If a diamond does not have these qualities, you may want to look closer to find out why.

Inclusions

Almost every diamond has inclusions. An inclusion is a small imperfection within the stone. Think of it as a birthmark or a fingerprint. Most diamonds are formed naturally underground, under extreme pressure and heat, over a long period of time. It's to be expected that they would have a few tiny flaws. The problem comes when these inclusions are clustered together in the stone. If that happens, your diamond can look cloudy or foggy.

What these inclusions do is block the light; it can no longer enter the stone and be reflected back to the one viewing it. It's the same with us. If we have 'flaws' or sins that we allow to remain in our lives, they can block the Light. Christ can no longer shine through our lives. No matter how much we try to clean up the outside of our lives, if we don't deal with the sin at the root of our problem, the cloudiness remains. Like Cain we may claim innocence and distance ourselves from reality, none of the coverups are potent enough to redeem us.

We are told,

> *You are the light of the world—like a city on a hilltop that cannot be hidden. No one lights a lamp and then puts it under a basket. Instead, a lamp is placed on a stand, where it gives light to everyone in the house. In the same way, let your good deeds shine out for all to see, so that everyone will praise your heavenly Father.* **(Matthew 5:14-16)**

> [7] *But if we walk in the light, as he is in the light, we have fellowship one with another, and the blood of Jesus Christ his Son cleanseth us from all sin.* **(1 John 1:7)**

> [6] *For God, who commanded the light to shine out of darkness, hath shined in our hearts, to give the light of the knowledge of the glory of God in the face of Jesus Christ.* **(2 Corinthians 4:6)**

Fluorescence

Fluorescence is defined as the characteristic of absorbing light that has a short wavelength and giving off light that has a longer wavelength. Some diamonds will actually glow in the dark when under a UV light. It sounds cool, but this added feature can cause them to appear milky when viewed in natural light.

God's word is true and complete; we shouldn't add to it. There are some people who want to augment Scripture with their own thoughts and ideas. Whether by flowery words and speeches or completely radical ideas, they try to tack on things that simply were not meant to be there. These things will cloud the message of the Gospel and inhibit its potency.

There are many places in the Bible that warn us not to add to God's word. For instance, in Proverbs 30 it says,

> *Do not add to his words, or he may rebuke you and expose you as a liar.* **(Proverbs 30:6)**

Dirt

In the course of time, the diamond has gotten dirty. If it's something that is worn every day, like a wedding ring, it's pretty easy for that stone to get dirty. It goes through things like gardening, dusting, hand lotion; you name it. If it doesn't get cleaned on a regular basis, it's going to start looking dull.

In the same way, we can allow our lives to get covered with dirt and crud. God's light has a hard time entering our hearts to transform us. His light cannot radiate through our lives if we are covered and messed up with dirt. Just like a diamond needs to be cleaned regularly, so do we. We need to allow God's word to wash us clean.

> *I have hidden your word in my heart, that I might not sin against you.* **(Psalm 119:11)**

We need to stop sinning, do what is right, and turn to God.

> *Wash yourselves and be clean! Get your sins out of my sight. Give up your evil ways. Learn to do good. Seek justice. Help the oppressed. Defend the cause of orphans. Fight for the rights of widows. Come now, let's settle this, says the Lord. Though your sins are like scarlet, I will make them as white as snow.* **(Isaiah 1:16-18a)**

We need to meet together with other believers.

> *And let us not neglect our meeting together, as some people do, but encourage one another, especially now that the day of his return is drawing near. **(Hebrews 10:25)***

We need to confess our sins to God.

> *For if we confess our sins to him, he is faithful and just to forgive us our sins and to cleanse us from all wickedness. **(1 John 1:9)***

We should not be of two minds, serving both God and the world.

> *Come close to God, and God will come close to you. Wash your hands, you sinners; purify your hearts, for your loyalty is divided between God and the world. **(James 4:8)***

We should not pollute our lives with filthy images.

> *They will never again pollute themselves with their idols and vile images and rebellion, for I will save them from their sinful backsliding. I will cleanse them. Then they will truly be my people, and I will be their God. **(Ezekiel 37:23)***

Finally, we need to remember that it is the blood of Jesus which cleanses us from our sins.

> *But if we are living in the light, as God is in the light, then we have fellowship with each other, and the blood of Jesus, his Son, cleanses us from all sin. **(1 John 1:7)***

Cracks

Even though diamonds are one of the hardest substances known to man, they can crack. If that weren't the case, how would they ever be cut into the size and shape we want? When a diamond cracks, it can make a portion of the diamond appear cloudy.

If you paid attention in school, you might remember lessons about the erosion that can happen as a result of water seeping into cracks in rocks. That water may seem harmless, but when the temperature drops, the water freezes and expands making the crack larger. When the temperature rises enough, the ice melts. The fluctuations in temperature can cause the process to repeat itself until, finally, the rock is broken.

As human beings, we are flawed. It's not uncommon to have 'cracks' in our lives. It may be a weakness or inadequacy in our lives. It may be an overt sin. Whatever it is, these cracks can allow sin to seep in. They may seem insignificant and harmless at first, but over time they will cause the cracks in our lives to widen until we break.

David had a crack, an unbridled love for women. Initially, it doesn't look like a crack because the excuse of royalty seems to rationalize his appetite for gathering a harem of wives. This growing weakness became matured the day all necessary ingredients for sin were made available to him. He couldn't stop himself, until he had crossed the borders of impurity and impunity; he seared and sealed his conscience. David took an ignoble step and gave heartwrenching order; Uriah was killed with the sharp sword of David's lust. Consequently, David bought and brought Bathsheba to his palace, the price was blood.

Those cracks can keep God's light from shining through us. If we allow sinful images, attitudes, and thoughts into our minds and hearts, then they will make us stray from God's presence and purpose. Instead, we should do what Philippians 4:8 tells us to

> *Fix your thoughts on what is true, and honorable, and right, and pure, and lovely, and admirable. Think about things that are excellent and worthy of praise.* **(Philippians 4:8)**

Diamonds In The Rough

DIAMOND NEEDLE

CHAPTER THREE

THE DIAMOND NEEDLE

How can you think of saying to your friend, 'Let me help you get rid of that speck in your eye,' when you can't see past the log in your own eye? Hypocrite! First get rid of the log in your own eye; then you will see well enough to deal with the speck in your friend's eye. **(Matthew 7:4-5)**

Do you know the difference between an industrial diamond and diamonds that are used in jewelry? Industrial diamonds are diamonds that have such severe imperfections in them that they are not worthy of being used as a gemstone. Believe it or not, only around 20% of diamonds which are mined ever make it as gems in jewelry. Even in gemstones, however, flaws exist.

Both in Biblical and contemporary times, there are several Bible characters whose imperfections were removed by God and they went on to do great and mighty works for in God's Kingdom.

JEPHTHAH: FROM SHAME TO HEROISM

Now Jephthah of Gilead was a great warrior. He was the son of Gilead, but his mother was a prostitute. Gilead's wife also had several sons, and when these half brothers grew up, they chased Jephthah off the land. You will not get any of our father's inheritance, they said, for you are the son of a prostitute. So Jephthah fled from his brothers and lived in the land of Tob. Soon he had a large band of rebels following him. (Judges 11:1-3)

Jephthah was the son of a harlot. Being a product of such parental defect is the worst thing that can happen to anyone in the Old Testament. It is a gross social and spiritual disgrace. God had earlier banished bastards from entering His house for worship, irrespective of their beauty or handsomeness.

Bastards suffered physical and spiritual rejection. Despite the graciousness of our God; surprisingly, he decided not to be merciful to any bastard. This was a law in Israel, even prayer could not change it. Any bastard bore a viral stigma of rejection.

Jephthah was excluded from having a lot or inheritance in his father's house. It was a state of emptiness and nakedness, hopelessness and failure. He endured and grew amidst rejection and mental torture. No child cherishes rejection, as rejection only precipitates evil habits and other social vices in any child. This happened to Jephthah; consequently, he joined men of questionable characters. Remember, evil association corrupts good manner.

At the zenith of rejection, Jephthah fled from home. This revealed how cruel the battle was at home. At every juncture where he needed parental guidance and support, he was denied.

Jephthah had a forgiving heart, when his people turned to him for help, he only requested assurance of their motives and commitment. After getting it, he went along with them and obliged their request. Indeed, all things work together for good to them that love God **(Romans 8:28).** A wise man once said, nothing is as bad as it first appears. Jephthah and his evil friends who were formerly rejected became a veritable battalion of deliverance for holy people.

Unholy people delivered holy people, unworthy men delivered worthy men, vagabonds delivered sons and a supposed bastard delivered heirs. He became the epitome of heroism. Indeed, no man can receive a thing except it is given to him from heaven. All of Jephthah's feats were products of grace and divine intervention. God made it happen.

JOHN MARK: GEM FROM THE FURNACE OF DISAGREEMENT

> *After some time Paul said to Barnabas, Let's return to each city where we previously preached the word of the Lord, to see how the new believers are getting along. Barnabas agreed and wanted to take along John Mark. But Paul disagreed strongly, since John Mark had deserted them in Pamphylia and had not shared in their work. Their disagreement over this was so sharp that they separated. Barnabas took John Mark with him and sailed for Cyprus. Paul chose Silas, and the believers sent them off, entrusting them to the Lord's grace. So they traveled throughout Syria and Cilicia to strengthen the churches there.* **(Acts 15:36-41)**

A great door of opportunity for evangelism, mentorship and exposure were opened for John Mark. Thank God for Barnabas' strong determination to ignore his inadequacies and take him along. Although, Mark's character defect as a deserter prompted resistance from Paul, these gross inefficiencies of Mark are instability and unfaithfulness.

Mark was as unstable as water; his indecision was colossal. These deficiencies almost cost him a golden opportunity in his ministerial life, but thanks be to God for Barnabas. Previously, Mark had accompanied Paul and Barnabas to Pamphylia. He handled the evangelistic mission childishly and deserted them. Mark was a disciple with little difference from Judas Iscariot. Consequently, Apostle Paul observed these flaws in Mark; therefore he denied him the invitation to follow them in the evangelistic tour.

Thank God for a patient leader (mentor) like Barnabas, he molded a faulty protégé to become an attractive and useful vessel. Mark was worked upon and he became a stable, trusted and dependable servant of Christ who could handle knotty matters.

> *Only Luke is with me. Bring Mark with you when you come, for he will be helpful to me.* ***(2 Timothy 4:11)***

An unprofitable servant became a profitable assistant and special instrument in evangelism and soul winning. Mark became a figure of faith that can stand for Christ and his mentors irrespective of any odd and opposition.

ONESIMUS: MY SON IN BOND

> *My plea is that you show kindness to Onesimus. I think of him as my own son because he became a believer as a result of my ministry here in prison. Onesimus hasn't been of much use to you in the past, but now he is very useful to both of us. I am sending him back to you, and with him comes my*

> own heart. *I really wanted to keep him here with me while I am in these chains for preaching the Good News, and he would have helped me on your behalf. But I didn't want to do anything without your consent. And I didn't want you to help because you were forced to do it but because you wanted to. Perhaps you could think of it this way: Onesimus ran away for a little while so you could have him back forever.* **(Philemon 1:10-15)**

Onesimus was a slave who ran away from his master. Ordinarily, only a gross misconduct could have made a slave abscond from the master in Onesimus' manner. Apostle Paul's choice of words further strengthened the thought that Onesimus must have done something grievous.

Through Paul, Onesimus became transformed and transfigured to the point that Apostle Paul vouched for him and was ready to pay any price just to see him grow. He became Paul's bond son. He was lost for a season, but forever regained for the advancement and establishment of God's kingdom on earth.

Finally, Onesimus became profitable to his master Paul and to himself. Formally, he ran away from responsibilities, but later, he was fully ready and willing to execute whatever task he was saddled with. He departed as a servant, but returned as a beloved brother with a burning passion and zeal for the Lord. There is something special in us that can skew an irrelevant man to the peak of relevance. This makes drawing conclusion on a man the most foolish task on earth.

It is a known fact, that diamonds are crystals. Some diamonds have crystals that form inside of the diamond as a whole. There are many types of these diamond crystals. One example is a needle. You probably guessed, thanks to its name, that a needle is a diamond crystal that is long and thin. They are caused by the extreme pressure that is placed on the diamond as it forms. In essence, the inclusion is smashed flat. A needle cannot form along one plane, say vertically, so it forms in another, say horizontally. Often a needle inclusion is very small and invisible to the naked eye.

People frequently form in the same way too. We are virtually under pressure on every noble facet of our lives; family, finance, ministry, career, etc. We cannot grow in the direction that we want to, so we are forced to go in a different direction. Sometimes the results of this pressure are obvious; sometimes they are not. It doesn't mean that it is necessarily a bad thing; it's just the evidence of our response to the pressures of life.

Joseph did not have traveling to Egypt on his to-do list. Jealousy bought a ticket for him, despite the trials, pains and luggage of complexities and uncertainties hurled at him he fulfilled God's will for his life.

At times inclusions like this can be truly lovely. They can combine to form beautiful shapes. Although they are usually colorless or a shade of white, they can be almost any color—green, black, gray, or red.

There are people who will ignore the huge 'log' in their own lives and try to point out the 'speck' in your life. When that happens, we each have another choice; how do we respond to this pressure? We can recoil, stop trying, decide that they are right and we are not good enough to go on. Jesus would probably have done lesser than He did, if he had allowed the noise and distraction of the Pharisees in His earthly ministry.

There was no single scriptural account where the Pharisees healed a simple headache, but there are numerous accounts of how they tried stopping Jesus from performing major miracles. No thanks to their unwholesome doctrines and spiritual blindness. We all have a strong decision to make whether we will go on and achieve our dreams or allow the "Pharisees" of our world to stop us. Just like Jesus, fulfilling God's ordained purpose should be our desire and utmost goal. We could also realize that no mortal is perfect, hence, we need God in every step of the journey.

We can accept that God can make something beautiful out of us despite or perhaps because of our imperfections. As Ecclesiastes 3:11 says,

> *God has made everything beautiful for its own time. **(Ecclesiastes 3:11)***

Diamonds In The Rough

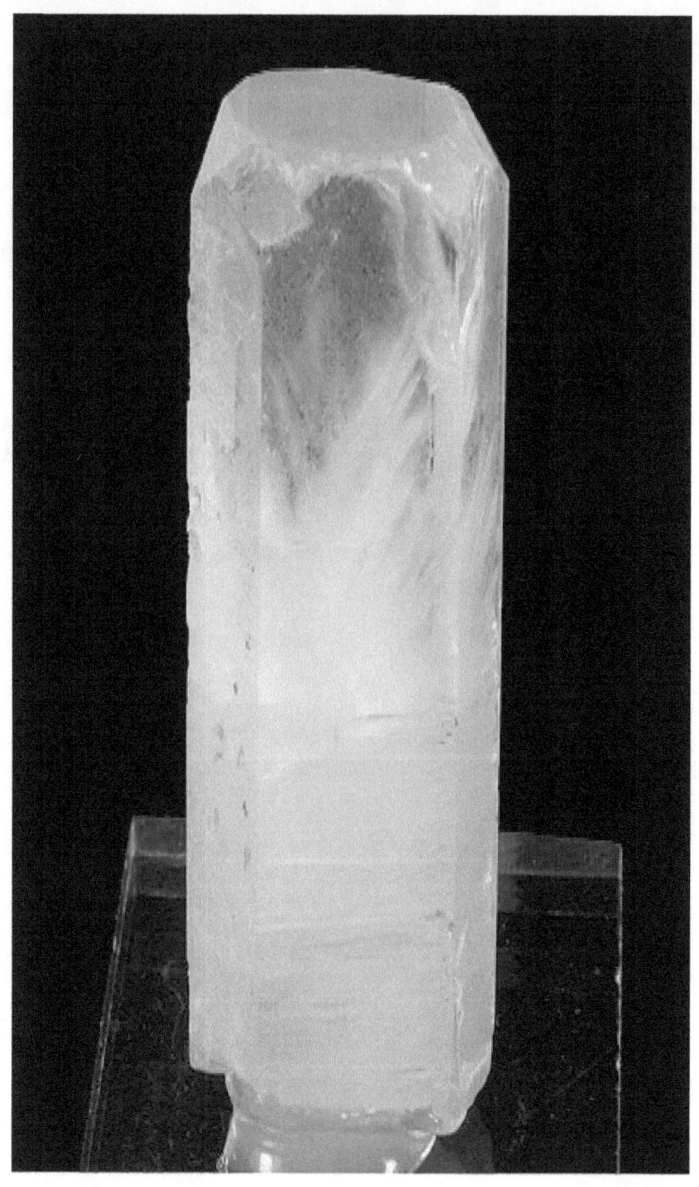

FEATHER DIAMOND

CHAPTER FOUR

THE FEATHER DIAMOND

A diamond with feather inclusions is one with tiny cracks that can resemble feathers. Most of these inclusions can be seen with a standard 10x jewelry loupe. They are usually white or perhaps transparent, but they do sometimes occur in other colors. Like most other inclusions, feather inclusions form when the diamonds are formed. They don't normally come from damage inflicted during the cutting process.

If a feather inclusion is buried deep in the stone, then it poses little risk to the gem. If a diamond has a feather inclusion that reaches all the way to the surface of the stone, it makes it more susceptible to damage.

Paul knew all about weaknesses and flaws. In 2 Corinthians chapter 12, we learned that Paul had something that he referred to as a thorn in the flesh. Whatever it was, he begged the Lord on three separate occasions to take it away. Each time that he asked, Jesus replied,

> *"My grace is all you need. My power works best in weakness." **(2Corinthians 12:9)***

Paul knew that God would not damage him, even if the cutting process was painful. Apostle Paul learned to let God use his weakness. He didn't let that weakness deter him or sit on the surface of his life and become a hindrance. Often, we will use our weaknesses as excuses. We often allow them sit on the surface of our lives and whenever we are asked to do something we claim that our weakness won't allow it. We let ourselves become broken and chipped instead of letting God use that weakness for His glory.

Here are some examples of people with weaknesses that God used:

Sarah

Sarah lived a long and full life. She served the Lord faithfully. She supported her husband in all his endeavors, even when it meant pulling up stakes and traveling into the unknown. Her heart pain was that she never bore children. In a society where a woman's worth was tied up in her family, Sarah was childless.

Sarah was already old when God promised Abraham that he would be the father of many nations. At the time of that promise, she was sixty-five. How thrilled she must have been! She followed her husband into a new land. Years passed, and she began to think that God had forgotten His promise. She started to scheme and figure out a way that she could force God's hand. Instead of waiting for God, she set a plan in motion that she felt would fulfill His promise.

The problem with this was that God had a plan all along. He knew that while it would be impressive for a seventy-six-year-old woman to have a child, it would be even more impressive for one who was ninety years old to give birth for the first time. He wanted to make sure that everyone knew that it was by His might and power that she had this child. He wanted to use what everyone around would view as a weakness for his glory.

Moses

What about Moses? When God first spoke to him and told him to speak to Pharaoh, Moses balked.

> *But Moses pleaded with the LORD, O Lord, I'm not very good with words. I never have been, and I'm not now, even though you have spoken to me. I get tonguetied, and my words get tangled.* ***(Exodus 4:10)***

Why do you think God asked Moses to be his emissary? Surely someone else would have been a better choice, even Moses' brother Aaron. Aaron spoke well according to the Lord.

Did God make a mistake when he chose Moses? Of course not, God knew all about Moses' insecurities. He also knew that by choosing someone who was less confident of himself and lacking in natural eloquence, it will become conspicuous to people that God can use anyone for His glory, including the weaklings. It is not about our power, but God's strength.

Rahab

Rahab was a renowned prostitute. Scripture did not reveal to us if she chose that life for herself or if it was chosen for her. What we do know is that when called upon to do what was right, she didn't use her flaws as an excuse to keep her from serving God. Not only did she allow God to use her, but God also turned her life around. Rahab left her life of prostitution and became a follower of the Lord. She married into the Israelite clan and became the great-grandmother of David. Jesus was one of her descendants.

Peter

Apostle Peter deserves a special mention. Peter was a fiery and interesting individual. Whatever he did, he did with passion. He walked on water, reprimanded Jesus; spoke out when he should remained silent, attacked those who came to take Jesus, and later denied Jesus.

Peter could have given up after denying Christ. He could have hung his head in shame, gone back to fishing and stayed there, but he didn't. He was impulsive, and it could have been a severe hindrance to the gospel, but God worked in Peter's life. After Jesus' resurrection Peter served God with his whole heart and life. Never again do we see it recorded that he got in the way of what God was trying to do. God used Peter's passionate nature for His glory.

The casual observer can often see feather inclusions in a diamond, just as the casual observer can see many of the weaknesses in our lives. The beauty lies in how the one who shapes the gem has decided to use that weakness. Do you use your weakness as an excuse to do nothing, or as an opportunity to show God's power?

Diamonds In The Rough

DIAMOND CHIP

CHAPTER FIVE

THE DIAMOND CHIP

A diamond chip is not the same as a chipped diamond. A diamond chip is the by-product of the cutting process. This term depicts the small pieces that chip off from the diamond as the gemcutter works to shape the rough diamond into the finished gem. It is not symmetrical; it is not faceted as a traditional gem would be, in fact, it is not even very attractive. A diamond chip doesn't have the sparkle of a finished gem because the only light it can reflect is off of its surface, it doesn't have the faceted depths of the finished product.

Having said all of this you might think that diamond chips are completely worthless or useless. That is not the case. Years ago, these tiny pieces were used as a complement to the main gem in a piece of jewelry and now, thanks to advancements in technology in the gem cutting field, even these tiny chips can be faceted to a certain extent.

Just as nothing was left to waste when cutting a diamond, God lets nothing go to waste in our lives. He knows what He is doing.

Think of the story of Joseph. He knew that God had big plans for his life. He had visions of grandeur, of his family bowing down before him. That had to have puffed him up a little. God gave him those visions so that he would have a dream for the future to hold onto, but He knew that he would have to chip away at that pride until the only thing that was left was the beautiful gem.

Look at all of the things that Joseph had to endure. He was thrown away and sold into slavery by his own brothers. He was falsely accused of attempted rape. He was imprisoned and forgotten. All of this happened before he was finally raised up into a position of authority second only to the ruler of Egypt. He became Pharaoh's right-hand man.

Finally, when there was a great famine in the land, Joseph's brothers came to buy food for their families. Joseph was only seventeen years old when his brothers sold him into slavery, a mere boy. Now he was thirty, a man. His brothers didn't recognize him. After all, who could have expected this bizarre turn of events? When they realized who stood before them in the place of power, they were understandably afraid. They literally threw themselves on Joseph's mercy. Joseph's reply shows how God used every part of the cutting process in his life. Joseph said,

> *You intended to harm me, but God intended it all for good.* **(Genesis 50:20)**

How many times in the Bible does God use small, seemingly insignificant things to do impressive feats? Look at Moses' humble shepherd's staff. It was used to part the Red Sea, bring water from a rock in the desert, and it even turned into a snake to impress those in Pharaoh's court and show God's power. A paltry stick became something powerful through God.

The widow in Zarephath allowed God to use the tiny bit of flour and oil that she had left to bring Him glory. She had planned to use it to fix a barely adequate last meal for herself and her son, but God had bigger plans. God stretched those provisions so that they not only had enough for that meal but for every meal that they would need from then until the drought ended and the crops grew again.

What about the little boy and his lunch? His mother had packed his lunch carefully before he left for the day. The boy followed Jesus and watched His miracles as he healed the sick in the crowd. When it was time to feed the crowd, the boy didn't hesitate; he offered his own food. He didn't question just how five loaves of barley bread and two fishes would multiply to feed all those people. He had witnessed Jesus doing the impossible all day. He knew that Jesus could use something as meager as tuna salad sandwiches to do a work that people would talk about for thousands of years.

> *God chose things despised by the world, things counted as nothing at all, and used them to bring to nothing what the world considers important. (***1 Corinthians 1:28)**

Even when it seems as if nothing good could possibly come from the smaller or seemingly ugly events in our lives, God has great plans for them. The little and despised town of Nazareth is a testament of this truth, God favored Nazareth and it became a worthy place and the town of Jesus Christ. God can use anything for His glory. We just need to be willing to let God do wonders with our lives. Will you allow God work on your diamond chip?

Photo by Shannon McInnes on Unsplash

CRACKED DIAMOND

CHAPTER SIX

A CRACKED DIAMOND

Then Samson prayed to the LORD, sovereign LORD, remember me again. O God, please strengthen me just one more time. ***(Judges 16:28)***

What happens to a diamond that has become cracked? You might think that it is ruined. Usually, that isn't the case; if a crack is small enough it might go unnoticed. A jeweler may be able to hide a tiny crack underneath the prong of a mounting so that no one discovers it. Some cracks are more substantial and need more attention. Sometimes the cracked stone will need to be re-cut and re-polished in order to become a brilliant gem once again. The new gem will be smaller than the original. It won't be what the gemcutters originally envisioned when they first saw that rough stone, but it will be valuable nonetheless.

Diamonds are a type of crystal. Their structure allows the professional diamond cutter to shape the rough stone into a finished gem. A blow at the precise spot and angle will result in a fracture. Unfortunately, this also means that despite being one of the hardest materials known to man, they can be cracked and broken under the right circumstances.

Some Christians seem almost as strong and invincible as a diamond. Sometimes they start to think of themselves that way. What happens when they become shattered and battered by the blows of this world? Do they crack or do they remain strong? If they have built their lives on the firm foundation of God's Word, then they will be able to stand, even if everything is crumbling around them. However, if they have been building upon other less sturdy foundations, they will crumble, crack, and fall along with everything else.

Peter was a typical example of believers who profess their invincibility.

> *Peter declared, Even if everyone else deserts you, I never will. Peter, Jesus replied, the truth is, this very night, before the rooster crows, you will deny me three times. No! Peter insisted. Not even if I have to die with you! I will never deny you! And all the other disciples vowed the same. Then Jesus brought them to an olive grove called Gethsemane, and he said, Sit here while I go on ahead to pray.* **(Matthew 26:33-36)**

Peter, at this stage of spiritual growth represents the group of mechanical believers; all that they do is in the flesh. Peter was convincing Jesus, telling Him how solid he would stand by Him during His dark hours of trials and pains. Peter's boast was underwritten by human zeal. It would have been better if he had backed his words with prayer. Jesus took him and two others to the garden called Gethsemane to pray in preparation for His imminent suffering and death. Alas! They snored and slumbered. Consequently, the scary reality of what Peter earlier boasted about rudely woke him up. Since they had slept while they should have been praying; one of them cut the ear of those who came to arrest Jesus. Finally, boastful Peter was measured on the scale of trial; quicker than expected, he denied Jesus, not once or twice but thrice.

> *A little later some other bystanders came over to him and said, you must be one of them; we can tell by your Galilean accent. Peter said, I swear*

> by God, I don't know the man. And immediately the rooster crowed. Suddenly, Jesus' words flashed through Peter's mind, before the rooster crows, you will deny me three times. And he went away, crying bitterly. **(Matthew 26:73-75)**

Instead of claiming an invincible stance before God, why not tell how incapable and weak we are? Unlike Peter who retraced his steps with much tears, why can't we openly call for mercy before our time of need?

Sometimes, Christians start out with good intentions. We love the Lord, read our Bible daily, pray and attend church services faithfully. We know that we are strong because we depend on God and His might and power. We are building our lives on a firm foundation.

Somewhere along the line, we begin to slack off. Our love has grown lukewarm at best. We read our Bible when it doesn't interfere with our television time. We pray when we remember. We attend church services if we're not too tired. We begin to think that we are strong in ourselves, that we don't need God quite as much. We have started to build our lives on a shaky and melting foundation.

An example of this was seen in the life of Samson. His life was dedicated to the Lord even before he was conceived. At a young age, the Spirit of the Lord began to stir him. He was not just strong, he was also filled with wisdom.

> And the child grew and became strong; he was filled with wisdom, and the grace of God was on him. **(Luke 2:20)**

As an adult, Samson began to wander from the ways in which he had been raised. He set his heart on marrying someone who did not serve the Lord. He became a victim of anger on several occasions. Although, God allowed Samson to preside as judge over Israel for twenty years; when Samson chose the wrong woman to love, and he thumbed his nose at the source of his power, God relegated Samson. His life finally cracked.

Samson learned so late that he could not continue to wink at sin, yet go scot free. He could not ignore God's commands, live his life on his own terms, and still expect God's blessing. He saw that his power was not his own. He came to realize that the only true power comes from God. When he turned to God at the end of his life, God used him for a final time. Although his life had been cracked, God was still able to use it for His glory.

Diamonds In The Rough

THE TWINNING WISP

CHAPTER SEVEN

THE TWINNING WISP

A diamond crystal can sometimes stop in its formation due to poor conditions, and then resume years, centuries, or millennia later. When the crystal formation picks back up, certain inclusions that began to form earlier can twist together with new inclusions, even if they are not the same type of inclusion. The good news is that most of these inclusions are small enough that they are not visible to the naked eye. A good gemcutter will cut a stone with a twinning wisp into a fancy cut diamond, following the natural lines and planes of the stone's inclusion as a guide. Pear, heart, and trilliant cut diamonds all fall into that category.

Every now and then, something will happen in a person's life that stunts their growth in a certain area. They may hide that unnecessary part of their lives away for years before opening up and beginning to grow once more. When they do, the growth may be bound up with other issues that have twisted around that first one. Does that mean that their lives will be ugly and twisted? They will become distorted only if they refuse to take appropriate steps. Let's take a look at Paul's life.

First, it was not uncommon for people of Paul's day to have two names. His Hebrew name was Saul, meaning 'prayed for.' This was the name that he went by in the Jewish community. He was well educated and respected. Acts chapter 7 reveals that as a young man he was a witness to the stoning of Stephen, a leader in the early church. Stephen was one of the men hand-picked by the original disciples to minister to the needs of the church. Acts chapter 8 begins with the chilling words,

> *Saul was one of the witnesses, and he agreed completely with the killing of Stephen. (Acts 8:1)*

Imagine this, Saul witnessed and approved the brutal stoning of this man. The chapter goes on to reveal that it was that event which inspired Saul to begin a crusade to annihilate the church. He went door to door dragging out both men and women to have them thrown in prison. The Scripture further revealed that he uttered threats against the believers with every breath and was eager to kill the Lord's followers. Nothing short of the voice of Jesus would have changed Saul's mind. Thankfully, Jesus intervened and spoke through a blinding light.

When Saul was on his way to Damascus to arrest more followers of Jesus, he was abruptly stopped by a brilliant light from Heaven and the voice of Jesus. Saul was struck blind, and for three days he fasted and prayed while waiting for the Lord's leading. When God's messenger, Ananias, came and laid hands on Saul and prayed for him, God restored his sight and Saul was filled with the Holy Spirit. God's mission for Saul was to herald the message of Jesus to the Gentiles, kings, and the people of Israel. When Saul took the gospel to the Gentiles, he began to use his Roman name, Paul, which meant small.

Saul had started out growing in one way, but his growth was cut short. Jesus stepped in, and Saul didn't know what to do, so he waited and asked for direction. God took this self-important 'prayed for' individual, and helped him to see just how 'small' he was. Once he was given that direction not only did he admit that he had been wrong, he also exerted as much energy into spreading the gospel as he had previously used while persecuting the Church of Christ.

We cannot afford to behave differently. Our innate characters that we will develop as we journey through life can be used in different ways. We each have a choice to make. Do we follow Christ or continue on our self-made paths? Once we begin growing again, we can allow God to skew those characteristics we once used for evil, for His glory and kingdom. Just as God used Paul's stubbornness and zeal for His glory, He can convert our private mess to global messages if we allow Him. The choice is ours to make, it is strongly suggested that you allow God to work on you, and become receptive to His will and leading for your life.

CERTIFIED DIAMOND

CHAPTER EIGHT

THE CERTIFIED DIAMOND: DIAMOND THAT HAS RECEIVED SALVATION

A diamond that has been certified has had its quality evaluated and approved by an independent professional gemological laboratory. A certificate will register the diamond's unique characteristics. The certificate will list the diamond's color, carat weight, clarity, and cut. It will also include a hand-drawn map of the stone's inclusions. No two diamonds are alike, so if one needs to verify which gem they are looking at, check the certificate. A diamond certificate says that the stone is no longer just a rough stone, but a gem. There are still inclusions and flaws; nonetheless, it is a gem.

How are we to become "certified"? In other words, what are the acceptable indicators that succinctly make anyone say, "I am a Christian"? There was a religious leader in the Bible named Nicodemus, who posed a similar question. He could see that Jesus had been sent by God to teach, but he lacked the understanding of how to become saved. Jesus told him that he had to be born again to enter the Kingdom of God.

All of us are born into this world, first physically. There is a reality that is coupled with the carnality and physicality of our birth. Indeed, it is a messy affair.

> *For I was born a sinner, yes, from the moment my mother conceived me.* **(Psalm 51:5)**

There will be pain, torture, torment, tears and everlasting punishment to anyone who misses Heaven. If we want to see God in Heaven, we must be born again, this time in the spirit.

Jesus had to endure pain, the anger of others, joy, and tears. The resultant effect of what Jesus endured was our new life and salvation. All we need to do is to believe in Jesus and accept Him as our Lord and Savior. We must believe in every part of Him; His miraculous birth, sinless life, teachings, death, resurrection from the dead and accompanying power.

Jesus tells us that,

There is no judgment against anyone who believes in him. But anyone who does not believe in him has already been judged for not believing in God's one and only Son **(John 3:18)**.

Not believing in Jesus is a choice – worst choice, but why would anyone choose not to believe? People make that choice because they love darkness more than light **(John 3:19)**. People who choose darkness over light love their lifestyle of sin. They are not willing to embrace the new life of Christ. They want to keep sinning.

They choose not to come to God's light because they are afraid **(John 3:20)**. Those who avoid the light and skulk around in the shadows fear what will happen when others see their depravity. Truthfully, they do not love darkness, but they have lived there for so long that they are afraid of the unknown. They are unsettled about what could happen to them if they come into the light of God. They are as well afraid of what others will say. Be informed, people will definitely say something. The opinion of any man should not make you a candidate of eternal doom.

Those who choose to come to the light do not do so because they are perfect. In fact, they are not, their imperfections brought them. They know that they are dirty and need to be cleansed. They have decided to come to the light in spite of all odds – disregarding the fact that their sins may be exposed. When they do so, others will see and affirm that they are doing what God wants. When they do so, they do so with the confidence that God will not punish them for their sins as they deserve because He loves them.

> *He has removed our sins as far from us as the east is from the west. The LORD is like a father to his children, tender and compassionate to those who fear him.* **(Psalm 103:12-13)**

Just as a diamond has its individual quirks and flaws, so do Christians. None of us is perfect on this side of eternity. We know that, and because His perfect love casts out all fear **(1 John 4:18)**, we should not be afraid to admit it. Our "certification" (salvation) comes from believing in Jesus Christ.

TRANSFORMED DIAMOND

CHAPTER NINE

THE TRANSFORMED DIAMOND: THE REFILLING OF THE HOLY SPIRIT

We have beamed our searchlight at why a diamond might need to be reshaped or remounted. Chips and damage might prompt someone to get a diamond repaired. Fads and fashion change over the years too. What was once considered vogue, attractive and useful becomes obsolete with time. (Women have seemingly outgrown the use of hat pins.)

When the Holy Spirit comes into a person's life, He may need to reshape, refill, refresh, and repurpose their lives as well. When we come to the light of Christ Jesus, we are saved. Although, we are not supposed to just sit contentedly on that gift. We have been tasked with the responsibility of telling people about Jesus **(Mark 16:15).**

> *But when the Holy Spirit has come upon you, you will receive power and will tell people about me everywhere, in Jerusalem, through-out Judea, in Samaria, and to the ends of the earth. (Acts 1:8)*

God did not recruit us without enabling us, He gave us the necessary tools to with which to work. In order to be used by God, we need to receive the power of the Holy Spirit, to be thoroughly equipped for this work.

On the day of Pentecost, seven weeks after Jesus' resurrection, the believers were meeting together in one place. Suddenly, there was a sound from heaven like the roaring of a mighty windstorm in the skies above them, and it filled the house where they were meeting. Then, what looked like flames or tongues of fire appeared and settled on each of them. And everyone present was filled with the Holy Spirit and began speaking in other languages, as the Holy Spirit gave them this ability **(Acts 2:1-4).**

In fulfillment of Jesus' promise, the Holy Spirit came down and filled some brethren who were gathered as instructed by Jesus. While they gathered and prayed, the Holy Spirit gave them utterance and they spoke in other languages. This gift was not just for show, but a veritable tool for evangelism. During this period of time, Jerusalem was the center of the modern world. People from different nations and languages often visited Jerusalem for assorted purposes. There were at least sixteen different languages recorded in this passage. The Holy Spirit made it possible for everyone to hear the message of the gospel in their own language. This pointed to the fact that Jesus died for all; and His gospel cannot be inhibited by language barriers or distance.

In our contemporary world, there are multitudes of different ways to spread the gospel. Options include sharing the good news with your neighbor, taking a Sunday school class, heralding it on your social media platform and evangelical missions across the nations of the world. The method employed is inconsequential; the willingness to go is more sacrosanct. Are you willing to be 'reshaped' so that God can use you?

Growing in the word of God

> *You must crave pure spiritual milk so that you can grow into the fullness of your salvation. Cry out for this nourishment as a baby cries for milk. (1 Peter 2:2)*

Growth is one of the characteristics of living things. Interestingly, we have not been called to a dead life, but new life. This implies that our new life in Christ is expected to grow just like every other living things. Nevertheless, as important as growth is, it is dependent on several other factors. The appropriate synergy of these contributing factors team up to orchestrate growth.

One important element necessary for growth is nutrition, simply say food. Food lubricates the engine of life. Food plays a major role in the growth of living things. Affirmatively, growth is subject to food. Permit me to say, no food--no growth.

This physical truth is in tandem runs parallel with spiritual laws. No Christian can grow without a balanced spiritual diet. The quality of spiritual food will determine the quality of growth. The word of God is our spiritual food. As physical food nourishes and enhances our bodies, so also, the word of God gives spiritual vitality and precipitates growth. Grace, faith, increase, prosperity, anointing, healing, safety, empowerment and lots more are all embedded in the Word.

> *So then faith cometh by hearing, and hearing by the word of God. **(Romans 10:17)***

This verse seemingly displays the word of God like a gate, when the gate is opened; faith and other spiritual graces are released for believers. Graciously, **Psalm 119:130** corroborates this thought,

> *The entrance of thy words giveth light; it giveth understanding unto the simple. **(Psalm 119:130)***

Figuratively, at the gate (entrance) of God's word, light is also given. Interestingly, do you know that until this gate is opened, you can never enjoy certain dimensions of blessings or experience certain heights in God?

> *Did you receive the Holy Spirit when you believed? he asked them. "No," they replied, we don't know what you mean. We haven't even heard that there is a Holy Spirit.* **(Acts 19:2)**

The sermon you have not heard can never bless you. This truth is responsible for the retardation and retrogression many believers are experiencing. What is the quality of the sermon or word you have been consuming? Your Spiritual walk cannot be better than the sermon you have listened to and the book you have read. This is one of the important reasons why new converts are encouraged to join Bible believing and teaching churches. Indeed, certain words can kill the growth of new converts. When the word is appropriately dispensed, it brings growth. Conversely, if it is wrongly preached, it can cause death. Indeed, the letter kills, but the word (spirit) gives life.

In Acts chapter 19 verse 2, some men could not enjoy the ministry of the Holy Spirit. Why? The gate of the word was closed. Until the arrival of Paul, men never knew there is another dimension of our walk with God that is empowered by the Holy Spirit. Any dimension of God that a minister of God lacks, will result in a suffering of the reality of that truth on his members.

It becomes imperative to ask, were these brethren excluded from enjoying the ministry of the Holy Spirit? No, but they were victims of spiritual malnutrition (the unspoken word).

All you need to live a fulfilled life in the world is the word. Until you find it, it cannot bless you.

It is advantageous to strike a balance here. One's whole scope of knowing God's word must not be hinged on your minister, Pastor or spiritual leader's sermons alone. Like the Berean believers, one must ensure to search the Scripture to know if those principles taught are correct.

> *Many will follow their evil teaching and shameful immorality. And because of them, Christ and his true way will be slandered.* **(2 Peter 2:2)**

Escaping the erroneous teaching of false prophets and heretic preachers is one of the reasons why we must know and understand God's written will on every matter. Otherwise, you will be tossed around by every wind of doctrine and philosophy. This was the instruction of God to Joshua.

> *Study this Book of the Law continually. Meditate on it day and night so you may be sure to obey all that is written in it. Only then will you succeed.* **(Joshua 1:8)**

The word of God if read, understood and applied will not only make you prosper, the knowledge will give assurance of the spiritual accuracy of what any other speaker or preacher teaches. The word of God is our spiritual capsule; it contains all vitamins and minerals that pertain to life and godliness. Neglecting it will make us become spiritually feeble, cachectic and stagnant. Let us prioritize the word of God.

Building a daily prayer relationship with God

Keep on praying. (1 Thessalonians 5:17)

The verse above is not a suggestion, it is a command. The frequency of prayer is nonstop, without breaks. Prayer is like breath in our nostrils. Our spiritual life is largely dependent on prayer. Hence, Apostle Paul commanded us to pray without ceasing. As we cannot live or survive physically without breathing, so it is spiritually with praying. The day we stop praying, we gradually fizzle out.

There is an important need to conscientiously build our prayer lives. Apostle Paul grew rapidly and excelled in ministry because he was a man of prayer.

*I thank God that I speak in tongues more than all of you. (**1 Corinthians 14:18**)*

He explored the potentials of prayer until he became one of the greatest apostles of all ages. He prayed more than all believers of his era, consequently, he became the brightest and most brilliant spiritual figure of his generation. **(Romans 12:12)**

The secret of any powerful Christian is prayer. This is a fact not open to debate, it is a gospel truth. Jesus expressly told His disciples, "this kind goeth not except by prayer and fasting." (**Matthew 17:20-22**)

Prayer is our secret as well as our weapon. Both in Biblical times and now, the results of prayer have always been humbling. It is correct to say, prayerlessness equals powerlessness, conversely, prayerfulness equals powerfulness.

Our requests today must echo the heart cry of Jesus' disciples, "Lord, teach us how to pray." When the grace is received, keep on praying.

Fellowshipping in the house of the Lord

> *And let us not neglect our meeting together, as some people do, but encourage and warn each other, especially now that the day of his coming back again is drawing near.* **(Hebrews 10:25)**

The power of God was given to the church not to individuals. This is so because Jesus died for all, not one. The church is the source of the great flow; wise believers know how to fetch from it.

> *"...O God, you are my God; I earnestly search for you. My soul thirsts for you; my whole body longs for you in this parched and weary land where there is no water. I have seen you in your sanctuary and gazed upon your power and glory".* **(Psalm 63:1-2)**

This is the loud cry of the man after God's heart. Earlier, King David had seen such wonder, glory, power, presence and manifestation that was rare. This had only happened in God's sanctuary hence, he was praying for a similar experience in his life. Wise Christians know that there are some deep manifestations of God which only occur during fellowship.

The Holy Spirit did not visit the disciples individually, despite knowing their individual addresses. He filled them while they waited on God in corporate prayer.

There is a tremendous power in togetherness. Two are better than one. One man will chase a thousand, but two put ten thousand to flight **(Deuteronomy 32:30).** Singleness can only seek addition, but togetherness will result in multiplication. The easiest time to kill any wild animal is when they walk alone, but when flocking in a group, their potential attackers refrain.

Jesus said, "Where two or three are gathered in my name, there I am in their midst". There is power in fellowship, power in corporate prayer and there is power in togetherness. Remember, until Jesus saw the multitude, He was not moved, but immediately when He saw them, He was moved with compassion.

> *Then if my people who are called by my name will humble themselves and pray and seek my face and turn from their wicked ways, I will hear from heaven and will forgive their sins and heal their land.* ***(2 Chronicles 7:14)***

Serving God

> *You must serve only the LORD your God. If you do, I will bless you with food and water, and I will keep you healthy. There will be no miscarriages or infertility among your people, and I will give you long, full lives. I will send my terror upon all the people whose lands you invade, and they will panic before you.* ***(Exodus 23:25-27)***

Nothing pays a greater dividend than serving God. It is possible to be a believer and not be committed to kingdom service. Serving God entails laying down your money, time, ambition and other things when due.

Many believers desperately want God's blessing, but in their ignorance, they have taken God for a fool. They are ever demanding and never giving. Serving God will interrupt certain good things in our lives, but the reward outweighs the act. **Exodus 23:25-26** gives a highlight of what God will take away from those who serve Him and the blessings that will be rewarded. He will take way sickness from you and He will blessed you to be bearing, with blessed food, water and long life.

It will interest you to know that we all eat, but only a fraction eats blessed food. Food blessed by God cannot cause diseases and illnesses. Have you ever wondered why the Israelites en route to Canaan, were not sick or feeble? The Lord blessed their food and water. Why? They served God. God had told Moses to lead the Israelites out of Egypt so that they could serve Him. As long as they remained faithful, God kept His promise of safety, provision and guidance.

God is seeking true worshippers that will worship Him in spirit and in truth. No eyes have seen what the Lord has in store for those who truthfully serve Him. Our success is directly contingent upon our service to the Lord. Our best sacrifice to God is not money but quality service.

Job and Abraham are perfect examples of faithful servants. At some points, their faith shook, there was displacement, they suffered delay, but after all, their services were generously rewarded by God. No service is lost in God's vineyard. God is not a debtor, whoever serves God, will be served by God in return. If you work for Him, He will work for you. If you walk with Him, He will closely attend to you.

When you listen and keep His laws, He will be attentive to your faintest whisper.

Teaching and Discipleship

> *Therefore, go and make disciples of all the nations, baptizing them in the name of the Father and the Son and the Holy Spirit. Teach these new disciples to obey all the commands I have given you. And be sure of this: I am with you always, even to the end of the age. **(Matthew 28:19-20)***

The importance of teaching and discipleship was underscored by Jesus. He emphasized it as one of His last commandments before He ascended to heaven.

There is nothing that we can do to please Him more than teaching and practicing discipleship. Our delay or neglect of this commandment magnifies our unprofitability.

We cannot afford to allow the sacrifice, blood and grace of Jesus to be wasted in our sinful neighbor's life. When we refrain from teaching others to become mature, we are disobeying Him.

The truth is, somebody taught and discipled us, it would be selfish to not reciprocate this act of kindness and love to others. What you know is not too little to share; some people don't know it at all.

The response of the Ethiopian eunuch "how can I understand except a man guide me" must spur us into action. Discipleship is about complete guidance. The spiritual lives of new converts, as well as other important facets of their physical lives, must come under the lens of discipleship and must be meticulously handled with all seriousness.

A poorly trained protégé will become a faulty mentor. Every deficiency skipped during training will affect his leadership life. If Paul could be trained and mentored in the desert of Arabia and if the cave of Adullam was maximized by David to train himself and others, none of us must shy away from training or deny other people training. The geographical scope of our teaching and practicing discipleship is the entire world. Do not limit your influence, there is more to do for the Lord. Go and make disciples of all men.

Walking in love

> *Love is patient and kind. Love is not jealous or boastful or proud.* ***(1 Corinthians 13:4)***

Although, our world daily fails the test of Love, but every believer should know that we have been called into the ministry of love. God is love; hence, we must love. Our salvation from darkness into His marvelous light is hinged on love.

> *For God so loved the world that he gave his only Son, so that everyone who believes in him will not perish but have eternal life.* ***(John 3:16)***

The same hand of love that God has extended to us, we must extend to others. Love is patient and kind, when people deserve it and when they don't. Love is the salt of life, without it, our world will become tasteless and rotten.

The summary of the law and the prophecy is love. Love has great power to promote and purify irrespective of the person's state. God saved us by using the tool of love to save the whole world. The saving power of love has not diminished; we must learn to engage in it. Most of the societal misdemeanors exhibited in our nation and families are quite unnecessary and avoidable, when we can walk in love.

Walking in love will bring great tranquility which has not been experienced both around and within us. If God is love, we must walk in love.

Diamonds In The Rough

PURPOSEFUL DIAMOND

CHAPTER TEN

SHINE LIKE A DIAMOND: THE PURPOSEFUL DIAMOND

Diamonds don't have any real purpose. In truth, they are just pretty rocks. Diamonds only find a purpose when they are taken out of their comfortable existence, shaped by a master's hands, and put to the use that an expert has in mind for them.

Some diamonds are used in an industrial setting. Since diamonds are extremely hard, they are occasionally used as an abrasive. Tiny particles of diamond can be molded into the blade of a saw, a grinding wheel, or a drill bit. Diamonds are also sometimes ground into powder and made into a polishing paste. Diamonds that are made into gems are actually cut and polished using tiny pieces of other diamonds. Diamonds can also be made into thin membranes called diamond windows that are used on x-ray machines and laser coverings. High-quality speakers can have thin domes made out of diamonds. The list goes on.

> No, O people, the LORD has told you what is good, and this is what he requires of you: to do what is right, to love mercy, and to walk humbly with your God. **(Micah 6:8)**

How will you know what is right? You need to have daily devotion, Bible reading, and prayer, along with fellowship with God and others in the house of the Lord.

> *I have hidden your word in my heart, that I might not sin against you.* **(Psalm 119:11)**

> *The heart of a man should not be empty, if it does not contain the right thing, definitely, the wrong acts and habits will spring forth from it. We must saturate our hearts with the word of God. This act helped Joseph when Potiphar's wife tried to ruin God's purpose for his life.*

> *But when you pray, go away by yourself, shut the door behind you, and pray to your Father in private. Then your Father, who sees everything, will reward you.* **(Matthew 6:6)**

> *And let us not neglect our meeting together, as some people do, but encourage one another, especially now that the day of his return is drawing near.* **(Hebrews 10:25)**

One of the greatest frustrations any man can experience is the ignorance of his life's purpose. When given the opportunity to have anything he wanted, Solomon chose to ask God for wisdom. As a result, he became the wisest man who ever lived before the arrival of Jesus. Solomon set out to learn all he could with his new-found wisdom.

> *But I learned firsthand that pursuing all this is like chasing the wind.* **(Ecclesiastes 1:17)**

Does this mean that our lives are futile or useless? No, it only reveals that when we vehemently chase worldly things, it's like chasing after the wind. The pursuit will never end because it is impossible to attain it. We should not try to live to please ourselves, for we will never be truly pleased or satisfied. No man, either dead or living, is created to please himself. What should we do? Here is Solomon's answer,

Here now is my final conclusion: Fear God and obey his commands, for this is everyone's duty.

> God will judge us for everything we do, including every secret thing, whether good or bad. **(Ecclesiastes 12:13-14)**

A deep thought about man and the rationale behind his creation will spur questions. (1) What did God have in mind for them to achieve? (2) What were they originally created to do?

For one thing, we were not created to be alone.

> *Then the LORD God said, "It is not good for the man to be alone. I will make a helper who is just right for him.* **(Genesis 2:18)**

It is interesting that one of the first things that was recorded about mankind is that we were created to help each other. We were never meant to bear our burdens alone. Be reminded,

> *A person standing alone can be attacked and defeated, but two can stand back-to-back and conquer. Three are even better, for a triple-braided cord is not easily broken.* **(Ecclesiastes 4:12)**

> *Exodus chapter 7 is a revelation of the fact that one man cannot do the work of God alone. As mighty and anointed as Moses was, he was helped by other people. Moses had Aaron to help him get God's message across to the people. Aaron and Hur held up Moses' hands when he was too weary to do it on his own.* **(Exodus 17:12)**

The book of Ruth unreservedly depicted the power of committed togetherness. Ruth left her family and homeland behind to be with Naomi. Ruth worked hard in a land where people were often unkind in order to provide for her aged mother-in-law.

In the book of Deuteronomy, we are admonished to be generous to the poor and needy in our land **(Deuteronomy 15:11).**

> *We were instructed to give to beggars and those who ask to borrow from us. **(Matthew 5:42)***

Matthew chapter 10 verse 8 teaches that we should use our gifts in helping other people.

> *For I was hungry, and you fed me. I was thirsty, and you gave me a drink. I was a stranger, and you invited me into your home. **(Matthew 25:35)***
>
> *Instead of storing up more than what we need, we are to give to the needy. **(Luke 12:33)***
>
> *We are to love as Jesus loved us. **(John 15:12)***
>
> *Those serving God should care for orphans and widows who are in need. **(James 1:27)***
>
> *We should work hard to provide for ourselves, our loved ones, and for people who are in need. **(Acts 20:34-35)***
>
> *If we are strong, then we should help others to do what is right. We should build them up. **(Romans 15:1-2)***

> *We are to help those believers back onto the right path who have been overcome by sin. We are to share each other's burdens.* ***(Galatians 6:1)***
>
> *Never think that you are too important to help other people.* ***(Galatians 6:3)***
>
> *We are to look and take good care of other people's property.* ***(Philemon 2:4)***
>
> *Ultimately, we are to lay down our lives for our friends.* ***(John 15:13)***

God didn't put people on Earth without giving them work to do. We may think that paradise would mean having nothing to do all day long, but we would be wrong. The first account of God's visit to earth revealed that He came to work. We are not serving a lazy God, and He won't accommodate laziness from us.

When God created human beings, he said that they would reign over creatures in the sea, air, and on the land. He created plants for the enjoyment of human-kind. God told Adam to tend and watch over all He had created.

Here are some things that the Bible tells us about work:

> *If we are lazy, we are as bad as someone who is actively destroying things.* ***(Proverbs 18:9)***
>
> *Someone who doesn't work because they are just too lazy will be poor, while a hard worker will be rewarded.* ***(Proverbs 10:4)***
>
> *Those who sleep when it's time to work are disgraceful.* ***(Proverbs 10:5)***

> *Lazy people will be ruined because they refuse to work.* ***(Proverbs 21:25)***
>
> *Too much sleep when there is work to be done will result in poverty.* ***(Proverbs 6:10-11)***
>
> *If we don't work, we must stay hungry.* ***(2 Thessalonians 3:10)***
>
> *Our work should have a purpose. We should work and train to be able to share the Good News and its blessings with everyone.* ***(1 Corinthians 9:22-27)***

God placed us on the earth to care for it. We must not be wasteful and reckless with respect to managing our resources without thoughts as to what lies ahead. Many verses in the Bible remind us of our responsibilities.

God created the earth and gave it everything that was needed; plants, trees that were both beautiful to look at and those that produced fruit, water, even gold and precious stones. Then God placed man in the garden so that he could tend it and watch over it.

He created animals as well, so that man could have companionship. We were meant to reign over them.

> *God tells us to look at the ants for inspiration. They have no leader, yet they work hard all through summer in preparation for winter.* ***(Proverbs 6:6-8)***
>
> *Scripture reminds us that the earth and everything that dwells there is the Lord's.* ***(Psalms 24:1)***

We know that God expects us to invest and properly use the resources that He entrusts to us. We need to remember that we are nothing without God. We can try to do good works, but they are meaningless without God. We should not allow ourselves to be deceived because every good and perfect gift comes from God. **(James 1:16)**

Jesus cautioned us to secretly practice charity, not public display. **(Matthew 6:1)**

We are reminded that, just as a branch doesn't produce fruit without the plant, we can do nothing without Jesus. **(John 15:4-5)**

Jesus patterned His life after God, He followed God's example. **(John 5:19)**

God created everything through Jesus. **(John 1:3)**

Even our very lives are not our own; it's the Lord who plots our course through life. **(Jeremiah 10:23)**

It is Christ who gives us the strength for what we need to do. **(Philippians 4:13)**

Everything that we do should be done in the name of the Lord Jesus. **(Colossians 3:17)**

Jesus warned us that if we try to do good outside of the will of the Father in Heaven, His verdict on us will be depart from me. **(Matthew 7:21-23)**

> *We should do nothing half-heartedly. We should work with enthusiasm and do it for the Lord.* ***(Colossians 3:23)***

> *We are told that God uses Scripture to prepare and equip us to do every good work.* ***(2 Timothy 3:16-17)***

> *It is God who works in and through us, giving us both the desire and the power.* ***(Philippians 2:13)***

We were made for fellowship with God. In the book of Genesis, God often came down to walk in the garden in the cool of the evening. It was man's sin that separated us from God and changed our fellowship. The point is, we were created to fellowship. God enjoys fellowship with us, and we were made to enjoy fellowship with Him.

Jesus' life was exemplary. The catch-phrase "what would Jesus do" became popular because it's a good way for us to figure out how we should act. Jesus didn't have one set of standards for himself and another set for His followers. Jesus was one of the busiest people there could be, yet he made time to fellowship with his Father. Imagine the very genuine claims on his time. People had legitimate needs. Jesus could easily have spent every minute of every day of his life here on earth teaching, healing, and helping people and still not have gotten to everyone. However, Jesus knew how important fellowship with his Heavenly Father was. Here are just a few examples:

> *Before Jesus began his ministry, he went out into the wilderness for forty days to pray and commune with God.* ***(Matthew 4, Mark 1, and Luke 4)***

*After the miracle of the five loaves and two fishes, Jesus sent his disciples on ahead, sent the people home, then went up into the hills alone to pray. **(Matthew 14:22-23)***

*He rose early in the morning, found a private place where he could be alone, and prayed. **(Mark 1:35)***

*It was the habit of Jesus to go to the Mount of Olives to pray. **(Luke 22:39-41)***

*Every time Jesus had a major decision to make, He went up on a mountain and stayed there all night praying. The next morning, he chose which of his followers would be his twelve apostles. **(Luke 6:12-13)***

*It is said that he often went into the wilderness to pray. **(Luke 5:16)***

*In what may have been his most difficult hours, his response was to pray. **(Matthew 26:36-42)***

We tend to think of a person's worth in terms of what they can do for us. Can this person advance our career? Will they help me out when I need it? What about the person who can do nothing for you? What about the person holding a sign at the intersection asking you for help? Do they have value? If everyone thought in those terms, the world would be a pretty sorry place.

Worse yet, what if God thought in those terms? God has everything; He lacks nothing **(Psalm 50:10).** In a day when a person's worth could be measured in how much livestock they owned, God let us know that He doesn't need our sacrifices. All of the animals of the forest belong to him. He owns the cattle on a thousand hills. When you think of it that way, what could we possibly have to offer Him? Does this mean that we are of no worth to God? Of course not! Let's look at a few of the Scriptures that tell us just how valuable we are to Him.

> *We were so carefully planned that God took the time and care to form us in our mother's womb. He knows every part of us. He had written out our days like a book before there was even one of them.* **(Psalm 139:13-16)**
>
> *God cares for the birds of the air, but we are more valuable to Him than they are.* **(Matthew 6:26)**
>
> *God is rich in mercy, so much so that he loved us even when we were dead in our sin. Thanks to Christ, we can be made alive and raised up to be seated in the heavenly places with Jesus. God wants to show us his grace and kindness in this way.* **(Ephesians 2:4-9)**
>
> *Jesus assured us that the Father knows when a single sparrow falls to the ground and that we are more valuable to God than an entire flock of sparrows.* **(Matthew 10:29b-31)**
>
> *We are precious, honored, and loved by God.* **(Isaiah 43:4)**
>
> *God loved each of us so much, that he gave his only Son so that we might live.* **(John 3:16)**

It is evident how worthy and valuable we are by what God went through and was willing to give up for us. When we see how valuable each soul is, we can begin to see why God gave us the Great Commission. **(Matthew 28:16-20)**

We are to go and make disciples of all nations. We are to teach these new followers of Christ to obey all the commands that Jesus gave us. Why? He did so because He loves us and wants the best for us. He did so because He wants us to live with Him for all eternity. Just as people stretch themselves to find, mine, and reshape diamonds, we should go to any length to pursue, teach and disciple others for Christ's kingdom.

A diamond is often cut, shaped, and polished by tools using other diamonds. In the same way, we as Christians should help shape and polish other Christians as one soul touches another. We should come alongside new Christians and help them. Again and again, we are encouraged to love one another as we were loved by Christ. Let us serve each other with love and kindness. We are to encourage each other, not discourage one another. We are to spur one another on toward love and good deeds. We should build each other up. We should teach each other. In Christ, we are all different members of the same body. Each member has its purpose, and each one exists to help and have equal concern for the others.

The 4 C's

First C - Cut

When people talk about diamonds, they talk about the four C's; that is cut, color, clarity, and carat. Cut speaks more to the proportions of the diamond rather than its shape. A diamond's cut determines its brilliance. Properly cutting and polishing a diamond allows the maximum amount of light to enter into the diamond through its top and to be reflected back the same way. If a diamond's cut is wrong, either too deep or too shallow, the light is lost through the bottom of the diamond; it is never reflected back.

When a person has not responded properly to life's storms, they exhibit the wrong "cut". They are either too shallow or they are too deep. If they are too shallow, they never dig deep enough into the wondrous things that God has for them. If they are too deep, they focus too much on their own pain and never look outward to the needs of others. Neither response is desired by God. God wants to shine His light on us, and He wants us to reflect that light both up and outward so that it can direct others to Him.

Do you remember Samson? He was a great example of someone who too shallow. Most of his life was lived to please himself. Rarely did he look to see how he could please God.

If you are looking for an example of someone who focused so much on his own pain without trying to meet the needs of others, you need to look no further than Jonah. When God told Jonah to speak to the people of Nineveh, he ran in the opposite direction. He had no love for those people. When God decided to spare Nineveh, instead of being happy for them, Jonah pouted and complained.

> *This change of plans greatly upset Jonah, and he became very angry. So he complained to the LORD about it: "Didn't I say before I left home that you would do this, LORD? That is why I ran away to Tarshish! I knew that you are a merciful and compassionate God, slow to get angry and filled with unfailing love. You are eager to turn back from destroying people. Just kill me now, LORD! I'd rather be dead than alive if what I predicted will not happen. (Jonah 4:1-3)*

Second C- Color

Although you might not realize it, diamonds come in virtually every color of the rainbow, everything from clear, yellow, blue, pink, purple, to almost black. Even though the most popular color is practically no color at all, any color is acceptable. For a diamond of color, the more intense the color is, the better.

The color of a diamond is synonymous with the spiritual gifts that each of us are given. Everyone's gift is unique. **1 Corinthians 12** tells us that there are different kinds of spiritual gifts, but they have the same Spirit as their source. Together we make up the body of Christ. Just because someone has a gift that is different from ours, doesn't mean that they should be despised or looked down on. Each gift, like each color, has a worth of its own.

> *God has given each of you a gift from his great variety of spiritual gifts. Use them well to serve one another. (1 Peter 4:10)*

Here are some patriarchs who used their spiritual gifts to serve others.

Paul recognized that Titus had the gift of administration. He felt fully confident leaving Titus in charge of appointing elders. **(Titus 1:5)**

Jacob had the gift of discernment in his latter years. Even without his physical sight, he could sense God's will when he was asked to bless his grandsons. **(Genesis 48:17-19)**

Paul is an excellent example of someone with the gift of evangelism. Some accounts of Paul's preaching can be found in the book of Acts.

Another of Paul's spiritual gifts was exhortation.

> *So we tell others about Christ, waring everyone and teaching everyone with all the wisdom God has given us. We want to present them to God, perfect in their relationship to Christ. That's why I work and struggle so hard, depending on Christ's mighty power that works within me. (Colossians 1:28-29)*

Abram (Abraham) had faith and followed God's leading without question. **(Genesis 12)** By serving God with his faith Abram (and others like him) showed us how to live and trust God.

Third C- Clarity

The clarity of a diamond is decided by how many flaws it has and exactly where they are located. Most diamonds have some flaws or inclusions. The diamond with no flaws whatsoever is extremely rare and valuable. Since inclusions affect how well light is reflected from the diamond, the fewer the inclusions, the better.

None of us is perfect. Each one of us has issues, flaws that affect our abilities to reflect the brilliant light of God. We need to allow God to help us to deal with our flaws so that we don't negate God's plan for our lives. Our purpose is to reflect God's Light in such a way that our lives bring men to Christ.

Gideon was full of fear. Even when God sent an angel down to tell him that God was going to use him to deliver Israel from the Midianites, he asked for one sign after another to be sure it was true. Despite his fear, Gideon finally permitted God to work through him, and became the mighty hero he was destined to be **(Judges 6:34).**

Fourth C- Carat Weight

Carat is a unit of weight used for measurement of precious stones such as diamonds. The more a diamonds weighs, the rarer it is. As you can imagine, a diamond of a larger carat weight is likely to be more valuable than a diamond of fewer carats. However, two diamonds can be of equal carat weight, yet have different values, thanks to their cut, color, and clarity.

Sometimes people will appear similar. They will have the same job, circumstances of birth and status, but how they have responded to different events, individual gifts, abilities and their flaws all affect the way that they can be used by God. In the end, all that counts are what we have done for the Lord.

Do not forget Joseph, his story of being sold into slavery by his own brothers, falsely accused of rape, imprisonment, and forgotten could have ended very differently if he had not allowed God to work in and through him **(Genesis 37-45).**

Daniel was a prince, yet he was captured and forced to become a servant. Daniel remained respectful and faithful. He never stopped serving the Lord no matter how difficult it became.

Paul was a learned fellow. If anyone had reason to boast about themselves, Paul's name should sit on top of such rating list. Yet he cared little for all of his earthly knowledge and accomplishments. He came to know that everything outside of Christ was worthless **(Philippians 3:8).**

Prayers

CHAPTER ELEVEN
PRAYERS

LORD SHOW ME MY PURPOSE

Father, I worship and praise your mightiness. I appreciate you for daily loading me with benefits. After the order of Apostle Paul, help me to know you more, O Lord. You created me for a purpose, Father reveal this purpose to me. I declare, I will not miss your plan for my life. Order my steps and perfect all than concerns me.

> *For I know the plans I have for you, says the LORD. They are plans for good and not for disaster, to give you a future and a hope.* **(Jeremiah 29:11)**

Shape and direct me appropriately. Let your light shine upon my path. Henceforth, I will not walk in darkness. I activate the ministry of angels; they shall minister grace, strength and protection to me.

You are the way, truth and the life. I shall enjoy great success, kingdom prosperity and the fulfillment of my purpose. Help my unbelief, strengthen my conviction and help to me have a restful confidence in you.

> *And we know that God causes everything to work together for the good of those who love God and are called according to his purpose for them.* ***(Romans 8:28)***

> *We can make our plans, but the LORD determines our steps.* ***(Proverbs 16:9)***

Show forth your glory in all my endeavors. I know that you are the God of all flesh; there is nothing that is impossible for you to do.

This confidence I have in you that you hear me at all times. I strongly believe you have put all that is necessary in motion to finally unveil my purpose.

I worship you O Lord. Forever will your name be praised. Amen.

A PRAYER OF GUIDANCE TO START A NEW DAY

Father, I thank you for the gift of life. Today is another day that the Lord has made; I will rejoice and be glad in it. I shake off failures, inadequacies and disappointments that have clogged my past. Today, I declare the grace of completion, helpers of destiny, showers of abundance and the opening of the floodgates of Heaven over my life, my ministry and my career.

Today, as I step out, the Lord will amplify my efforts. Every step that I take shall bring favor, honor, peace, help and ascension to greater height. After the order of Jesus at the mount of transfiguration, I put on the glory of God; my face shall radiate glory after the order of Moses. The Lord shall robe me with a new garment after the order of Joshua the priest. I go with thanksgiving, I shall return with testimony.

You who feed the sparrow shall see to my welfare. I shall lack no good thing. I receive grace to seek you first and the advancement of your kingdom. I decree, I shall be a comfort to the depressed, joy to mourners and healing to the wounded.

I declare, I will not stray out of your law and commandment. I receive the grace to modify my excesses and to be led at all times. Breathe grace and fulfillment on all I do. As I put you first in all I do, help me to love my neighbor as myself.

Give me the heart to let go and embrace peace today and beyond. Be the alpha of this day as well as the omega. Help me to keep your law even under the most stringent temptation. I receive grace to flee from every appearance of sin and enterprise that will deter me from becoming all that you have in store for me. Thank you for making me a son and joint heir with Christ. I cannot thank you enough for the supreme sacrifice of Jesus. Today, all the redemption benefits and packages are mine. As I go out today, I will radiate the life of the risen savior and Lord of my life.

Teach me to count my days and put my heart according to wisdom. Help me to make the best and maximize all opportunities that come my way. I declare, I shall live a life of praise and years of thanksgiving. Outside of you, I'm nothing; please help me cling to you all through the hours of today. Thank you, my loving savior. In Jesus' name I have prayed, Amen.

PRAYERS FOR INNER HEALING

The term inner healing refers to the healing of our thoughts and emotions. There are many things that happen to us throughout our lives over which we have no control. Some of those things can leave lasting scars. It is not wrong to want to be healed from those scars, but Christians need to guard ourselves from approaching such supposed solution wrongfully. There are practices that are used in other religions and movements that have begun to creep into the Church when it comes to dealing with these scars that are not biblical.

One such method is to visualize that event or events. Some of these 'visualization' techniques open a person up to evil forces that we are meant to avoid. We also are not meant to dwell on those things in our past. Romans chapter 6 tells us that our old lives and desires are dead and we now have new lives, thanks to Christ. Philippians chapter 3 admonishes us to forget the past and look to what lies ahead. We cannot win the race by always looking behind us. We must keep our focus on God, not ourselves.

Having said this, we shouldn't ignore our hurts and emotions either. We should acknowledge our feelings and come to God asking for help to deal with them appropriately. Slowly lean on this Word; it is renewing and healing.

> *Jesus is the way, the truth, and the life.* **(John 14:6)**
> *The truth will set you free.* **(John 8:32)**

> *The Spirit of the Lord will comfort the broken-hearted, and free captives.* **(Isaiah 61:1)**

> *God will heal the broken-hearted.* **(Psalm 147:3)**

*God will heal your wounds. **(Jeremiah 30:17)***

*The Lord will bring your soul out of its prison. **(Psalm 142:7)***

*The Lord is near to everyone who has a broken heart and a crushed spirit, and he rescues them. **(Psalm 34:18)***

*The Lord God will heal us when we cry out to him. **(Psalm 30:2)***

Dear Lord,

You see the hurt in my past. You know how deeply this has affected me and the way I see the world. I am a child of God and I have been washed with the blood of Jesus, and I know that He came to set me free. I claim that freedom right now. I know that He is near to the brokenhearted and a present help in the time of need. I know that the Lord will heal me when I cry out to Him, because He is the greatest Healer. So, I am crying out to you right now Lord and I ask you to heal me of the hurts and scars that have inflicted my past with pain. I pray that you take what was intended for harm in my life and use it for good. I ask this in Jesus' name.

Amen

Diamonds In The Rough

BIBLIOGRAPHY

Elliot, E. (2018, January 18). *"How can I know if God is leading me to become a missionary?"*. Retrieved from Ask a Missionary: http://www.askamissionary.com/question/16

Troutman, N. (2018, January 18). *To Live is Christ.* Retrieved from nenatroutman.com: http://www.nenatroutman.com/to-live-is-christ.html

When Americans Become Christian. (2018, January 21). Retrieved from Missions Mobilizer: http://home.snu.edu/~hculbert/ages.htm

NOTES

NOTES